Ace Your M

PERCENTS AND RATIOS

ACe your MatH TesT

Rebecca Wingard-Nelson

Enslow Publishers, Inc.
40 Industrial Road
Box 398
Berkeley Heights, NJ 07922
USA

http://www.enslow.com

Library of Congress Cataloging-in-Publication Data
Wingard-Nelson, Rebecca.
  Percents and ratios / Rebecca Wingard-Nelson.
     p. cm. — (Ace your math test)
  Includes index.
  Summary: "Learn about percents and ratios, including how to tell what's a better pur-
chase, figuring out sales tax and discounts and appropriate tips"— Provided by publisher.
  ISBN 978-0-7660-3781-6
  1. Ratio and proportion—Juvenile literature. 2. Percentage—Juvenile literature. 3.
Fractions—Juvenile literature. I. Title.
  QA117.W566 2011
  513.2'4—dc22
                             2010048198

Paperback ISBN 978-1-4644-0008-7
ePUB ISBN 978-1-4645-0457-0
PDF ISBN 978-1-4646-0457-7

Printed in the United States of America

092011 Lake Book Manufacturing, Inc., Melrose Park, IL

10 9 8 7 6 5 4 3 2 1

To Our Readers: We have done our best to make sure all Internet Addresses in this book
were active and appropriate when we went to press. However, the author and the publisher
have no control over and assume no liability for the material available on those Internet sites
or on other Web sites they may link to. Any comments or suggestions can be sent by e-mail
to comments@enslow.com or to the address on the back cover.

♻ Enslow Publishers, Inc., is committed to printing our books on recycled paper. The paper
in every book contains 10% to 30% post-consumer waste (PCW). The cover board on the
outside of each book contains 100% PCW. Our goal is to do our part to help young people
and the environment too!

Illustration Credits: Shutterstock.com

Cover Photo: Comstock/Punchstock

CONTENTS

Test-Taking Tips

Be Prepared!

Most of the topics that are found on math tests are taught in the classroom. Paying attention in class, taking good notes, and keeping up with your homework are the best ways to be prepared for tests.

Practice

Use test preparation materials, such as flash cards and timed worksheets, to practice your basic math skills. Take practice tests. They show the kinds of items that will be on the actual test. They can show you what areas you understand, and what areas you need more practice in.

Test Day!

The Night Before

Relax. Eat a good meal. Go to bed early enough to get a good night's sleep. Don't cram on new material! Review the material you know is going to be on the test.

Get what you need ready. Sharpen your pencils, set out things like erasers, a calculator, and any extra materials, like books, protractors, tissues, or cough drops.

The Big Day

Get up early enough to eat breakfast and not have to hurry. Wear something that is comfortable and makes you feel good. Listen to your favorite music.

Get to school and class on time. Stay calm. Stay positive.

Test Time!

Before you begin, take a deep breath. Focus on the test, not the people or things around you. Remind yourself to do your best, and not to worry about what you do not know.

Work through the entire test, but don't spend too much time on any one problem. Don't rush, but move quickly first, answering all of the questions you can do easily. Go back a second time and answer the questions that take more time.

Read each question completely. Read all the answer choices. Eliminate answers that are obviously wrong. Read word problems carefully, and decide what the problem is asking.

Check each answer to make sure it is reasonable. Estimate numbers to see if your answer makes sense.

Concentrate on the test. Stay focused. If your attention starts to wander, take a short break. Breathe. Relax. Refocus. Don't get upset if you can't answer a question. Mark it, then come back to it later.

When you finish, look back over the entire test. Are all of the questions answered? Check as many problems as you can. Look at your calculations and make sure you have the same answer on the blank as you do on your worksheet.

Let's Go!

Three common types of test problems are covered in this book: Multiple Choice, Show Your Work, and Explain Your Answer. Tips on how to solve each, as well as common errors to avoid, are also presented. Knowing what to expect on a test and what is expected of you will have you ready to ace every math test you take.

1. Ratios

A ratio is a relationship between two values that shows one value in terms of the other.

Ratios can be shown in different ways. If there are three hot dogs and one hamburger you could write ratios in the following ways:

- using a colon, as in 3 : 1 (for every three hot dogs, there is one hamburger)

- using the word "to," as in 3 to 1 or 3 hot dogs to 1 hamburger

- using the fraction bar, as in 3/4 are hot dogs and 1/4 are hamburgers

- as a single number that is found by dividing one value by the total, as in 0.75 are hot dogs (by dividing 3 by 4) or 75% are hot dogs (0.75 as a percentage)

Parts and Wholes

Four girls ate a total of 12 cookies: 3 oatmeal and 9 chocolate chip. What is the ratio of:
    a. girls to cookies
    b. oatmeal cookies to chocolate chip cookies
    c. oatmeal cookies to total cookies

Part a: This part of the problem compares two different whole values, the whole number of girls and the whole number of cookies. There are 4 girls and 12 cookies. Let's use the word "to" for this ratio. The ratio of girls to cookies is **4 to 12**.

Part b: This part of the problem compares two parts of the whole number of cookies. Part of them are oatmeal and part are chocolate chip. The girls ate 3 oatmeal cookies and 9 chocolate chip cookies. Let's write this ratio using a colon. The ratio of oatmeal to chocolate chip is **3 : 9**.

Part c: This part of the problem compares part of the cookies to the whole number of cookies. The girls ate 3 oatmeal cookies and ate a total of 12 cookies. Let's write this ratio using a fraction bar. The ratio of oatmeal to total is **3/12**.

Definition

term: A number in a ratio. The terms are named by where they appear in the ratio.

For example, in the ratio 1 : 4, the number 1 is the first term, and the number 4 is the second term.

When a ratio is written as a fraction, the top number is the first term, and the bottom is the second term.

TEST TIME: Multiple Choice

Mia made 13 quarts of strawberry jam and 5 quarts of peach jam. What is the ratio of strawberry jam to the amount of jam Mia made in all?

a. 13/5

b. 5/13

c. 5/18

d. 13/18

The problem does not tell you the amount of jam Mia made in all. Add the strawberry and peach to find the amount of jam in all. 13 + 5 = 18. She made 13 quarts of strawberry jam. This is the first term. She made 18 quarts in all. This is the second term. The ratio of strawberry to all is 13 to 18.

Solution: The correct answer is d.

Test-Taking Hint

Multiple choice problems give you a list of solutions. Other kinds of problems ask you to provide the solution. Problems that ask you to provide the solution should be answered clearly and in complete sentences.

Some problems ask a question and ask you to explain your answer.
Others just ask for an answer. Your score is based on both a
correct response and how clearly you explain your reasoning.
Include examples when they will clarify your answer.

TEST TIME: Explain Your Answer

Are ratios the same as fractions?

Solution: Ratios and fractions are not the same thing.
Some ratios are fractions, but not all.

Fractions always compare a part to the number of parts in one whole.
For example, if a class has 26 students, 12 boys and 14 girls, the
fraction of boys in the class is 12/26. This is also a ratio.

Ratios can compare two parts of a whole thing, a part to a whole, or
two completely different things. The ratio of boys to girls in the class
is 12/14. In this case, 12/14 is a ratio but not a fraction because 14
does not represent the whole.

2. Equivalent Ratios

Definition
equivalent: Equal in value.

Patterns

Patterns can help you understand equivalent ratios.
The following section of a pattern shows two pumpkins
and three leaves. The ratio of pumpkins to leaves is 2 : 3.

Continuing the pattern, there are now four pumpkins and
six leaves. The ratio is 4 : 6.

If the pattern were to continue for one more set, you
would have six pumpkins and nine leaves. The ratio of
pumpkins to leaves is 6 : 9.

Each of these ratios 2 : 3, 4 : 6, and 6 : 9 show the same
pattern. They are equal, or equivalent ratios.

TEST TIME: Show Your Work

A noodle recipe calls for a ratio of 3 cups of flour to 2 eggs. How many eggs are needed if you use 6 cups of flour?

The ratio of flour to eggs is 3 cups to 2 eggs. You can find an equivalent ratio by multiplying each term by the same number.

If the original flour term is 3 cups and the new flour term is 6 cups, the multiplier is 2.

    3 cups × 2 = 6 cups

Multiply the eggs term by the same number, 2.

    2 eggs × 2 = 4 eggs

Solution: You need 4 eggs.

Test-Taking Hint

Questions that ask you to find your own solution are sometimes called "Show Your Work" or "Short Answer" questions. Showing your work and showing some effort will earn you part of the credit, even if you have the wrong answer. The right answer, without showing some work, may only give you partial credit.

Actual Numbers

Ratios are sometimes best left as the original ratio.

Tim says a bus has 48 riders and 24 seats, so the ratio of seats to riders is 24 : 48. Is Tim correct?

Step 1: There are 24 seats. This is the first term. There are 48 riders. This is the second term.

$$24 : 48$$

Yes, Tim is correct.

Tina said the ratio of seats to riders is 1 : 2. Is Tina correct?

Step 1: Check to see if the ratios 24 : 48 and 1 : 2 are equivalent. You can multiply both of Tina's terms by 24.

$$1 \times 24 = 24 \quad 2 \times 24 = 48$$

Yes, Tina is correct.

Bill wants to know how many riders were on the bus. Will the ratio from Tim or Tina be better for his needs?

Step 1: Tina's ratio does not give enough information. Tim's ratio uses the actual numbers.

Bill should use Tim's ratio.

When you might need to know the actual numbers, do not rewrite a ratio in an equivalent form.

Which two ratios are equivalent?

A. 12 : 4   B. 2 : 8   C. 4 : 1   D. 16 : 4

          a. A and B
          b. B and C
          c. B and D
          d. C and D

In each of the ratios except B, the first term is greater than the second. Since none of the other ratios can be equivalent to B, eliminate each of the options that includes B. The only choice that does not include ratio B is answer d. Check answer d. Are 4 : 1 and 16 : 4 equivalent ratios? Yes.

Solution: The correct answer is d.

Test-Taking Hint
Some multiple choice questions can be solved by eliminating choices that are obviously incorrect.

3. Reducing Ratios

Multiply or Divide

Equivalent ratios can be found by multiplying or dividing both terms by the same number.

The ratio of class time to homework time is 4 hours to 12 hours. Find two equivalent ratios for 4 : 12.

Step 1: Find the first equivalent ratio using multiplication. Multiply both the first and second terms by 2.

$$4 \times 2 : 12 \times 2$$

$$8 : 24$$

Step 2: Find a second equivalent ratio using division. Divide both the first and second terms by 2.

$$4 \div 2 : 12 \div 2$$

$$2 : 6$$

4 : 12, 8 : 24, and 2 : 6 are equivalent ratios.

Test-Taking Hint

In multiple choice problems with the answer choice all of the above, it is best to check all of the choices.

TEST TIME: Multiple Choice

Which ratio is equivalent to 20 to 50?

          a. 10 to 25

          b. 4 to 10

          c. 2 to 5

          d. All of the above.

Check each answer to see if it is equivalent to the original ratio.

Answer a: The first term of the original ratio is 20, the first term of answer a is 10. To get from 20 to 10, divide by 2. When you divide the second term of the original ratio by 2, the result is 25.
10 to 25 is equivalent to 20 to 50.

Answer b: $20 \div 5 = 4$ and $50 \div 5 = 10$.
4 to 10 is equivalent to 20 to 50.

Answer c: $20 \div 10 = 2$ and $50 \div 10 = 5$.
2 to 5 is equivalent to 20 to 50.

Solution: Since answers a, b, and c are all correct, the correct choice is answer d, all of the above.

Definitions

factors: Numbers that divide evenly into a given number. The number 2 divides evenly into 6. The number 2 is a factor of 6.

common factors: Numbers that divide evenly into a set of numbers. The number 3 divides evenly into 9 and 12. The number 3 is a common factor of 9 and 12.

greatest common factor: The largest number that divides evenly into a set of numbers.

lowest terms: A ratio is in lowest terms when it cannot be reduced any more.

Test-Taking Hint

Some problems ask a question, and ask you to explain your answer. Others just ask for an explanation. Your score is based on both a correct response and how clearly you explain your reasoning. If there is no direct question, try to include an example when you can.

TEST TIME: Explain Your Answer

There are 27 boys and 36 girls on the track team. How can you find the ratio of boys to girls in lowest terms?

Solution: The ratio of boys to girls is 27 : 36.

You can write the ratio in lowest terms by dividing each of the terms by the greatest common factor.

The factors of 27 are 1, 3, 9, and 27.
The factors of 36 are 1, 2, 3, 4, 6, 9, 12, 18, 36.
The common factors of 27 and 36 are 1, 3, and 9.
The greatest common factor is 9.

$$27 : 36$$
$$27 \div 9 : 36 \div 9$$
$$3 : 4$$

In lowest terms, the ratio of boys to girls is 3 : 4.

4. Rates

Definition

rate: A ratio that compares two different kinds of quantities. Units are included when writing rates.

Rates are written in two ways:

    using the word "per", $20 per 3 pounds

    using the fraction bar, $20/3 pounds

Rates are always read using the word "per".

        "Twenty dollars per three pounds"

Find a Rate

Lupe is paid for the number of bookmarks she makes. Last night Lupe made 30 bookmarks and was paid $18. What is Lupe's rate of pay?

Step 1: Writing a rate is similar to writing a ratio. The only difference is that the units must be included. For a rate of pay, write the dollar value first.

        $18 per 30 bookmarks

TEST TIME: Multiple Choice

Ian worked 2 hours before lunch and 6 hours after lunch.
He earned $50 for the day. What was Ian's rate of pay?

          a. $50 per 6 hours
          ⓑ $50 per 8 hours
          c. $25 per 3 hours
          d. $25 per 2 hours

Ian worked both before and after lunch. Add the hours to find how many hours he worked for the day. He earned $50 for the day. The rate is $50 per 8 hours.

Solution: Answer b is correct.

Test-Taking Hint

Some problems will have the same answer in two places, just written in a different way. Answer a says the rate is $50 per 6 hours. Answer c says $25 per 3 hours. These are equivalent rates, but neither is correct.

Lowest Terms

Lupe made 12 beaded necklaces and was paid $24. What is Lupe's rate of pay in lowest terms?

Step 1: Write the dollar value as the first term. Remember to include the units.

$24 per 12 necklaces

Step 2: Reduce the rate to lowest terms by dividing each term by the greatest common factor, 12.

$24 ÷ 12 per 12 ÷ 12 necklaces
$2 per necklace

Test-Taking Hint

You can find the lowest terms of a ratio without using the greatest common factor.

Reduce the ratio by dividing each term by any common factor. Then reduce the new ratio by dividing each term by any common factor. Continue reducing until the terms have no common factors except 1.

TEST TIME: Show Your Work

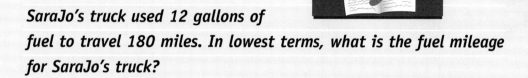

SaraJo's truck used 12 gallons of fuel to travel 180 miles. In lowest terms, what is the fuel mileage for SaraJo's truck?

Mileage is a special rate that compares the number of miles driven to the amount of fuel consumed.

Remember to write the answer in a full sentence.

Solution: The fuel mileage for SaraJo's truck is 180 miles per 12 gallons of fuel. Both terms can be divided by 6.

$$(180 \div 6) \text{ miles per } (12 \div 6) \text{ gallons}$$
$$30 \text{ miles per 2 gallons}$$

Both new terms can be divided by 2.

$$(30 \div 2) \text{ miles per } (2 \div 2) \text{ gallons}$$
$$15 \text{ miles per gallon}$$

SaraJo's truck mileage is 15 miles per gallon of fuel.

5. Ratios, Fractions, and Decimals

Definitions

multiple: The product of a number and any whole number. Multiples of 3 are 3, 6, 9, . . .

common multiples: Numbers that are multiples of two or more numbers in a group. Some common multiples of 2 and 3 are 6, 12, and 18.

least common multiple: The smallest multiple, other than zero, that two or more numbers have in common.

Whole Number Ratios

Ratios may have a term that is a fraction or a decimal, such as 1/3 to 3/4 or 1.2 to 1. Fractional and decimal ratios can be written as whole number ratios to make them easier to understand.

Write 1/3 to 1/2 as a whole number ratio.

Step 1: Find the least common multiple of the denominators.

The multiples of 3 are 3, 6, 9, 12, . . .
The multiples of 2 are 2, 4, 6, 8, 10, 12, . . .
The common multiples of 3 and 2 are 6, 12, 18, . . .
The least common multiple of 3 and 2 is 6.

Step 2: Multiply both terms in the ratio by the least common multiple of the denominator, 6.

$$1/3 \times 6 : 1/2 \times 6$$
$$2 : 3$$

TEST TIME: Show Your Work

For every 1 $^2/_3$ cups of peanut butter in a cookie recipe there is 1 cup of butter. Write a whole number ratio for the ratio of peanut butter to butter.

The amount of peanut butter is a fraction. The amount of butter is a whole number. When only one of the values is a fraction, multiply each term by the denominator.

Solution: The ratio of peanut butter to butter is 1 $^2/_3$ to 1.

$$1 \,^2/_3 : 1$$
$$1 \,^2/_3 \times 3 : 1 \times 3 \qquad \text{Rewrite the mixed fraction as}$$
$$^5/_3 \times 3 : 1 \times 3 \qquad \text{an improper fraction to multiply.}$$
$$5 : 3$$

Decimals and Powers of Ten

When a decimal is multiplied by a power of ten (such as 10 or 100), the decimal point moves to the right one place for each zero.

Multiply 3.987 × 1,000.

Step 1: There are three zeros in 1,000. To multiply by 1,000, move the decimal point in the other factor three places to the right.

$$3.987 \times 1{,}000 = 3{,}987$$

Test-Taking Hint

An answer in a multiple choice problem might look correct if you go too quickly. Read the question and look at the answers carefully. Often the wrong answers given are ones you would find if you made a common error.

TEST TIME: Multiple Choice

The ratio of wheat to oats in a cereal bar is 4.2 grams to 6.05 grams. Which of the following is the ratio of wheat to oats in lowest whole number terms?

> a. 42 : 605
> b. 420 : 605
> c. 84 : 121
> d. 84 : 103

The original ratio of wheat to oats is 4.2 : 6.05. The first term has one decimal place. The second term has two decimal places. Move the decimal point two places right by multiplying each term by 100.

$$4.2 \times 100 : 6.05 \times 100$$
$$420 : 605$$

Be careful. This is NOT the correct answer. The problem asks for the ratio in lowest whole number terms. Reduce the ratio to lowest terms by dividing each term by the greatest common factor, 5.

$$420 \div 5 : 605 \div 5$$
$$84 : 121$$

Solution: Answer c is correct.

6. Unit Ratios and Rates

Definitions

unit ratio: A ratio with a second term that is one unit, such as 2 students to 1 table.

unit rate: A rate with a second term that is one unit, such as 16 miles per 1 gallon.

Unit rates usually do not include the number one in the second term. Instead of saying 16 miles per 1 gallon, you say 16 miles per gallon.

Unit Ratios

An ice cream topping is made using 3 parts caramel and 2 parts fudge. Write the unit ratio for caramel to fudge.

Step 1: Write the original ratio of caramel to fudge.

$$3 : 2$$

Step 2: Write the ratio as a unit ratio. To convert any ratio to a unit ratio, divide each term by the second term.

$$3 : 2$$
$$3 \div 2 : 2 \div 2$$
$$1.5 : 1$$

The ratio of caramel to fudge is 1.5 to 1

TEST TIME: Explain Your Answer

Eric has 150 classic rock songs and 30 jazz songs on his favorite playlist. Write the ratio of classic rock to jazz and explain how you can tell how many times more classic rock songs there are than jazz songs.

Solution: The ratio of classic rock songs to jazz songs on Eric's favorite playlist is 150 to 30.

If you write the ratio as a unit ratio, it tells you how many times more the first term is than the second.

$$150 \div 30 \text{ to } 30 \div 30$$
$$5 \text{ to } 1$$

There are five times as many classic rock songs on Eric's favorite playlist as there are jazz songs.

TEST TIME: Show Your Work

When Bella works 12 hours, she earns $87.00. What is Bella's pay rate?

Problems that ask you to find a common rate, such as pay rate, are asking you to find the unit rate. Write the original rate of dollars to hours. Divide each term by the second term, the number of hours.

Solution: $87 per 12 hours

$87 ÷ 12 per 12 ÷ 12 hours

$$\begin{array}{r} 7.25 \\ 12\overline{)87.00} \\ -84 \\ \hline 30 \\ -24 \\ \hline 60 \\ -60 \\ \hline 0 \end{array}$$

$7.25 per hour

Bella earns 7.25 per hour.

Unit rates may have a fraction or decimal as the first term. The answer, $7.25 per hour, has a decimal as the first term.

Other Rates

Some rates are so common they have their own name. Mileage compares miles to amount of fuel. Density compares the number of items to how much space they take up.

What is the speed of a plane that travels 240 miles in 30 minutes?

Step 1: Travel speed is a rate that compares distance to time. Speed can compare any distance unit, such as miles, feet, or inches, to any time unit, such as hours, minutes, or seconds. Use the units that are given in the problem unless the question asks for different units.

240 miles per 30 minutes

Step 2: Find the unit rate. Divide each term of the ratio by the number in the second term.

240 miles ÷ 30 per 30 minutes ÷ 30
8 miles per minute

The plane's speed is 8 miles per minute.

Extras

Any rate that includes the word speed compares something to an amount of time. For example, typing speed compares the number of words typed to the amount of time it took to type them. When the word speed is used alone, it normally refers to distance over time.

7. The Better Buy

Definitions

price: The price of an item is usually given as the total cost of the item. For example, the price of a case of 24 bottles of water might be $6.55.

unit price: The unit price is the price for one measurement unit of an item. The measurement unit may be a unit of weight, such as a pound. It could also be a unit of volume, such as a liter. Sometimes a unit price is given per item. For example, you might buy 6 trees. The unit price is the price for one tree.

Unit Price

A 12-ounce can of soup costs $1.68. What is the unit price of the soup?

Step 1: Unit price is found in the same way as any other unit rate. Write the original price.

$$\text{\$1.68 per 12 ounces}$$

Step 2: Divide each term by the number in the second term.

$$\text{\$1.68} \div 12 \text{ per 12 ounces} \div 12$$
$$\text{\$0.14 per ounce}$$

The unit price for the soup is $0.14 per ounce.

TEST TIME: Multiple Choice

A six-pack of 12-ounce cans of cola costs $3.60. What is the price per ounce of cola?

> a. $0.60
> b. $0.30
> c. $0.06
> d. $0.05

This problem tells you to find the unit price in ounces. The original price is given for 6 cans of cola. Each can contains 12 ounces. One way to find the unit price is to first find the cost of one 12-ounce can, then find the price per ounce.

$3.60 per 6 cans	$0.60 per 12 ounces
$3.60 ÷ 6 per 6 ÷ 6 cans	$0.60 ÷ 12 per 12 ÷ 12 ounces
$0.60 per can	$0.05 per ounce

Solution: Answer d is correct.

TEST TIME: Show Your Work

A 6-ounce package of beef jerky costs $3.69.
A 20-ounce package of the same brand costs $11.80.
Which package is the better buy?

This problem is asking for the better buy, or lower unit price. Find and compare the unit prices for the two packages. You can use a calculator to divide the total price by the number of ounces in each package.

Solution: $3.69 per 6 ounces $11.80 per 20 ounces

$$\frac{\$3.69}{6} \text{ per } \frac{6}{6} \text{ ounces} \qquad \frac{\$11.80}{20} \text{ per } \frac{20}{20} \text{ ounces}$$

$0.615 per ounce $0.59 per ounce

The 20-ounce package is the better buy.

Test-Taking Hint

Some tests allow you to use calculators. Use a calculator when you know how to solve a problem. It will save you time you may need for other problems.

Comparing Other Rates

Any rates that have the same units can be compared.
Write each rate as a unit rate first.

Brenna drove 570 miles using 30 gallons of fuel. Sammi drove 352 miles using 16 gallons of fuel. Whose car gets better fuel mileage?

Step 1: Find the unit rate for each of the girl's cars.

Brenna: 570 miles per 30 gallons
570 ÷ 30 miles per 30 ÷ 30 gallons
19 miles per gallon

Sammi: 352 miles per 16 gallons
352 ÷ 16 miles per 16 ÷ 16 gallons
22 miles per gallon

Step 2: Compare the unit rates.

19 miles per gallon is less than 22 miles per gallon.
You want to get MORE miles per gallon.

Sammi's car gets better fuel mileage.

8. Distance, Rate, and Time

The Distance Formula

A formula is an equation that uses words or symbols to show how measurements relate to each other.

The distance formula shows the relationship between distance, speed, and time. The distance formula says:

$$\text{distance} = \text{speed} \times \text{time}$$

You can find how far something goes (distance) by multiplying how fast it moves (speed) by how long it takes to move (time).

Distance

Jeff rode his bike at a steady speed of 18 miles per hour for 1.5 hours. How far did Jeff ride?

Step 1: The distance formula tells you that if you multiply speed by time, you can find the distance traveled. Multiply 18 miles per hour by 1.5 hours.

18 miles per hour $\times$ 1.5 hours = 27 miles

Jeff rode his bike 27 miles.

TEST TIME: Multiple Choice

How long will it take you to walk 12 miles if you walk at a steady speed of 4 miles per hour?

  a. 3 minutes
  b. 3 hours
  c. 48 minutes
  d. 48 hours

This problem tells you the distance and the speed. It asks you to find the time. You can use the distance formula to understand the relationship between the measurements.

distance = speed × time

12 miles = 4 miles per hour × time

12 = 4 × time

To find a missing factor in multiplication, use division.

12 ÷ 4 = 3, so

12 miles = 4 miles per hour × 3 hours

Since speed is in miles per hour, time is also in hours.

Solution: Answer b is correct.

Converting Units

To convert from larger to smaller units, multiply by a whole number. The answer will be greater than the original value.

How many inches are in 6 feet?

Step 1: There are 12 inches in one foot. Inches are smaller than feet, so multiply the number of feet by the number of inches in one foot.

6 feet × 12 inches per foot = 72 inches

There are 72 inches in 6 feet.

To convert from smaller to larger units, divide by a whole number. The answer will be less than the original value.

How many yards are 27 feet?

Step 1: There are 3 feet in one yard. Yards are larger than feet, so divide the number of feet by the number of feet in one yard.

27 feet ÷ 3 feet per yard = 9 yards

There are 9 yards in 27 feet.

Test-Taking Hint

The units in a problem must match. If the speed is given in miles per hour, the time is also in hours. When units do not match, be sure to convert them.

TEST TIME: Show Your Work

Jackie drove for 30 minutes at a steady speed of 40 kilometers per hour. How far did Jackie drive?

Use the distance formula.

Solution: distance = speed × time

distance = 40 kilometers per hour × 30 minutes

Since the units in speed are in kilometers per hour, convert the time units from minutes to hours. Minutes are smaller than hours, so divide the number of minutes by the number of minutes in one hour, 60.

30 minutes ÷ 60 minutes per hour = 0.5 hours

Replace the minute units with the hour units and multiply.

distance = 40 kilometers per hour × 0.5 hours

20 kilometers = 40 kilometers per hour × 0.5 hours

Jackie drove 20 kilometers.

9. Proportions

Definition

proportion: An equation showing two equivalent ratios. Proportions are normally written using two fraction bars.

$$\frac{1}{2} = \frac{3}{6}$$

Proportions are also written using colons. 1 : 2 = 3 : 6

Proportions are always read using the words "is to" and "as."

"One is to two as three is to six."

There are four terms in a proportion. They are named by their position.

$$\frac{\text{first term}}{\text{second term}} = \frac{\text{third term}}{\text{fourth term}}$$

Writing Proportions

Write a proportion using the ratio 2 : 5.

Step 1: Find an equivalent ratio using multiplication or division. Multiply both the first and second terms by 2.

$$2 \times 2 : 5 \times 2$$
$$4 : 10$$

Step 2: Write the ratios as a proportion.

$$2 : 5 = 4 : 10$$

TEST TIME: Explain Your Answer

Are the ratios 4/7 and 32/56 proportional? Explain your answer.

This problem asks if the ratios are proportional. This is the same as asking if the ratios are equivalent. Since the problem uses the word *proportional*, write the ratios as a proportion. A true proportion will have equivalent ratios. If the ratios are not equivalent, the proportion is said to be NOT true.

Solution:

$$\frac{4}{7} = \frac{32}{56}$$

One way to check for equivalent ratios is to reduce each ratio to lowest terms. The first ratio is already in lowest terms. Reduce the second ratio by dividing each term by 8.

$$\frac{4}{7} = \frac{32 \div 8}{56 \div 8} \qquad\qquad \frac{4}{7} = \frac{4}{7}$$

The proportion is true, so the ratios are proportional.

Definitions

cross multiply: To multiply the diagonal terms in a proportion. Multiply the first term by the fourth term and the second term by the third term.

cross product: The result of cross multiplication. The cross products in a proportion are equal.

$$\frac{\text{first}}{\text{second}} = \frac{\text{third}}{\text{fourth}} \qquad (\text{first}) \times (\text{fourth}) = (\text{second}) \times (\text{third})$$

Cross Products

Use cross products to show that $\frac{3}{5} = \frac{9}{15}$ is a true proportion.

Step 1: Write the proportion.

$$\frac{3}{5} = \frac{9}{15}$$

Step 2: Cross multiply.

$$3 \times 15 = 5 \times 9$$
$$45 = 45$$

The cross products are equal, so the proportion is true.

TEST TIME: Multiple Choice

Which proportion is NOT true?

a. 12 : 1 = 24 : 2
b. 6 : 18 = 1 : 3
c. 4 : 5 = 25 : 20
d. 2 : 3 = 8 : 12

This problem asks you to find the proportion that is not true.
Three of the four ARE true.

One way to solve this problem is to find the cross products for
each proportion. The one that is NOT true is the correct answer.

a. $12 \times 2 = 24 \times 1$, $24 = 24$ True
b. $6 \times 3 = 18 \times 1$, $18 = 18$ True
c. $4 \times 20 = 5 \times 25$, $80 = 125$ NOT True
d. $2 \times 12 = 3 \times 8$, $24 = 24$ True

Solution: Answer c is not true, so it is the correct answer.

Test-Taking Hint

When a question is taking an especially long time, or
has you stumped, leave it and go on. Come back later if
you have time.

10. Solving Proportions

Mental Math

Finding a missing term in a proportion is called solving the proportion. In simple proportions, you can use mental math to find the missing term.

Find the missing term.

$$\frac{1}{6} = \frac{5}{\blacksquare}$$

Step 1: You can solve a proportion by finding equivalent ratios. To change the first term, 1, to 5, you multiply by 5. Do the same to the second term, 6.

$$1 \times 5 = 5$$
$$6 \times 5 = 30$$

Step 2: Write the complete proportion.

$$\frac{1}{6} = \frac{5}{30}$$

Test-Taking Hint

Not all of the questions on a math test need computations. Know math definitions and know the reasons behind the math.

TEST TIME: Multiple Choice

A proportion is an equation that shows _____.

    (a.) equivalent ratios
    b. equivalent terms
    c. like ratios
    d. like terms

Some multiple choice questions ask that you fill in a blank with the most appropriate words. Read the question carefully and choose the BEST answer.

In this problem, all of the answer choices use words that are related to proportions, but only one answer is correct.
A proportion shows that ratios are equivalent.

Solution: The correct answer is a.

TEST TIME: Show Your Work

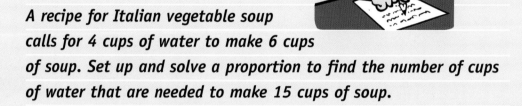

A recipe for Italian vegetable soup calls for 4 cups of water to make 6 cups of soup. Set up and solve a proportion to find the number of cups of water that are needed to make 15 cups of soup.

This problem gives you directions on how to solve the problem. To get full credit, you need to follow the directions by setting up and solving a proportion.

The ratio given is cups of water to cups of soup. Set up a proportion of water to soup.

Solution: water $$\frac{4}{6} = \frac{?}{15}$$ soup

In proportions, the cross products are equal. Cross multiply.

$$4 \times 15 = 6 \times ?$$
$$60 = 6 \times ?$$

You need to find the number that can by multiplied by 6 for a product of 60. Divide 60 by 6.

$$60 \div 6 = 10$$

water $$\frac{4}{6} = \frac{10}{15}$$ soup

You need 10 cups of water to make 15 cups of soup.

The Shortcut

Find the missing term.

$$\frac{3}{4} = \frac{?}{16}$$

Step 1: You can find a missing term in any proportion in two steps. Multiply, then divide. Cross multiply the two terms that are both given.

$$\frac{3}{4} = \frac{?}{16} \qquad 3 \times 16 = 48$$

Step 2: Divide the cross product by the known term that is left. The result is the unknown term.

$$\frac{3}{4} = \frac{?}{16} \qquad 48 \div 4 = 12$$

$$\frac{3}{4} = \frac{12}{16}$$

11. Ratios in Geometry

Definition

similar figures: Figures that have the same shape, but not necessarily the same size.

Similar Figures

A rectangle is 2 inches wide and 5 inches high. A similar rectangle is 4 inches wide. How tall is the second rectangle?

Step 1: Similar figures have corresponding measurements that are in proportion. Set up a proportion for the measurements of the similar rectangles.

$$\text{width} \atop \text{height}$$ $$\frac{2}{5} = \frac{4}{?}$$

Step 2: Cross multiply the terms that are both known.

$$\frac{2}{5} = \frac{4}{?} \qquad 5 \times 4 = 20$$

Step 2: Divide the cross product by the known term that is left. The result is the unknown term.

$$\frac{2}{5} = \frac{4}{?} \qquad 20 \div 2 = 10$$

The second rectangle is 10 inches tall.

TEST TIME: Multiple Choice

Triangle A is similar to triangle B. What is the length of the missing side?

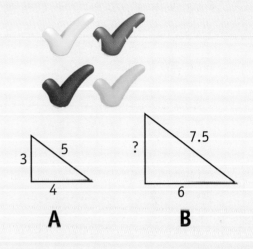

a. 4.0

(b.) 4.5

c. 8.0

d. 10.0

In similar figures all of the corresponding sides are in the same ratio. You can use any pair of corresponding sides with given measurements to find the missing measurement.

Set up a proportion relating triangle A to triangle B.

Triangle A
Triangle B

$$\frac{4}{6} = \frac{3}{?}$$

Multiply, then divide.

$$3 \times 6 = 18$$
$$18 \div 4 = 4.5$$

Solution: The correct answer is b.

Reduce First

Ratios in a proportion can be reduced to lower terms before you cross multiply.

Find the missing term.

$$\frac{25}{100} = \frac{?}{12}$$

Step 1: Reduce the ratio to lowest terms. Remember, reducing does not change the value of the ratio. Divide each term in the first ratio by 25.

$$\frac{25 \div 25}{100 \div 25} = \frac{?}{12}$$

$$\frac{1}{4} = \frac{?}{12}$$

Step 2: Cross multiply the terms that are both known.

$$\frac{1}{4} = \frac{?}{12} \quad 1 \times 12 = 12$$

Step 3: Divide the cross product by the known term that is left. The result is the unknown term.

$$\frac{1}{4} = \frac{?}{12} \quad 12 \div 4 = 3$$

$$\frac{25}{100} = \frac{3}{12}$$

TEST TIME: Explain Your Answer

*A 20-foot tree casts a
shadow that is 30 feet long.
Next to the tree and at the same time, a man casts a shadow that
is 9 feet long. How tall is the man? Explain how you know.*

Solution: The heights of objects and the lengths of their shadows are
proportional when they are measured at the same time of day. You can
find the height of the man by setting up a proportion.

	tree		man
height in feet			
shadow length in feet	$\dfrac{20}{30}$	$=$	$\dfrac{?}{9}$

Reduce the first			
ratio to lowest terms.	$\dfrac{2}{3}$	$=$	$\dfrac{?}{9}$

Multiply.	$2 \times 9 = 18$
Divide.	$18 \div 3 = 6$

The man is 6 feet tall.

12. Scale Models

Definition

scale: A ratio that compares the measurements of a type of representation, such as a drawing or model, to the measurements of the object it represents. The representation is always the first term. The measurement of the actual object is the second term.

Maps

On a building map, the door to the science lab is 3 inches from the exit of the building. The map scale is 1 inch to 10 feet. How far is the science lab door from the exit of the building?

Step 1: The scale tells you that on the map 1 inch is the same as 10 feet in actual distance. You can find missing measurements that use a scale drawing using a proportion. Use the scale as the first ratio. Fill in the part of the second ratio that you know.

scale inches
actual feet

$$\frac{1}{10} = \frac{3}{?}$$

Step 2: Solve the proportion by finding equivalent ratios.

$$\frac{1 \times 3}{10 \times 3} = \frac{3}{30}$$

The science lab door is 30 feet from the exit.

TEST TIME: Multiple Choice

A map scale is 1 centimeter = 50 miles.
The actual distance between Sydney's home and his first vacation stop is 375 miles. How far apart are Sydney's home and his first stop on the map?

a. 7.5 centimeters
b. 75 centimeters
c. 7.5 miles
d. 75 miles

Set up a proportion and solve it.

$$\text{map centimeters} \atop \text{actual miles} \quad \frac{1}{50} = \frac{?}{375}$$

Cross multiply and divide.

$1 \times 375 = 375 \qquad 375 \div 50 = 7.5$

The solution is map distance. It is in centimeters.

Solution: The correct answer is a.

Test-Taking Hint

Scales are sometimes given using the equal sign.
1 inch = 10 miles means that one inch on the model is 10 miles in real distance.

Definitions

reduction: A scale that creates a model that is smaller than the original object.

enlargement: A scale that creates a model that is larger than the original object.

Enlargements

A digital picture is enlarged to show details at a scale of 2 cm = 1 mm. In the original picture, a man's nose is 0.75 mm long. What is the length of his nose in the enlarged picture?

Step 1: Set up a proportion. Use the scale as the first ratio. Fill in the part of the second ratio that you know.

scale centimeter
original millimeters
$$\frac{2}{1} = \frac{?}{0.75}$$

Step 2: Cross multiply the terms that are both known.

$$\frac{2}{1} = \frac{?}{0.75} \qquad 2 \times 0.75 = 1.5$$

Step 3: Divide the cross product by the known term that is left. The result is the unknown term.

$$\frac{2}{1} = \frac{?}{0.75} \qquad 1.5 \div 1 = 1.5$$

The man's nose is 1.5 cm long in the enlargement.

Test-Taking Hint

When you don't feel confident about an answer, and have time, try solving it a different way. That way, you are less likely to make the same mistake twice.

TEST TIME: Explain Your Answer

Is the scale 1 meter = 0.2 cm a reduction or an enlargement? Explain your reasoning.

Solution: A scale that is a reduction makes the model smaller than the original. An enlargement makes a model that is larger than the original. The first term in a scale ratio is the model. The second term is the original.

If the first term is the smaller term, the scale is a reduction. If the first term is the larger term, the scale is an enlargement.

One meter is larger than 0.2 centimeters, so this is an enlargement.

For example, if an item is 0.2 centimeters long, the scale model will be 1 meter long. The model is larger than the original item. This is an enlargement.

13. Alternate Proportions

Definition

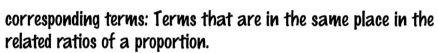

corresponding terms: Terms that are in the same place in the related ratios of a proportion.

$$\frac{\text{first term}}{\text{second term}} = \frac{\text{third term}}{\text{fourth term}}$$

The first and third term are corresponding terms.
The second and fourth term are corresponding terms.

Correspoding Terms

What are the corresponding terms in the ratio
1 : 4 = 3 : 12?

Step 1: Look at the ratios on each side of the equal sign.

The first term in the ratio on the left is 1. The first term in the ratio on the right is 3. These are corresponding terms.

1 and 3 are corresponding terms.

The second term in the ratio on the left is 4. The second term in the ratio on the right is 12. These are corresponding terms.

4 and 12 are corresponding terms.

TEST TIME: Show Your Work

Find the missing term, then name
the corresponding terms.

$$\frac{2}{3} = \frac{?}{21}$$

Solution: Cross multiply and divide to find the missing term.

$$2 \times 21 = 3 \times ?$$
$$42 = 3 \times ?$$
$$42 \div 3 = 14$$

$$\frac{2}{3} = \frac{14}{21}$$

2 and 14 are corresponding terms. 3 and 21 are corresponding terms.

Test-Taking Hint

Pay more attention to the question you are working on
than to the amount of time left for the test.

Definition

alternate proportion: A proportion using the corresponding terms as the ratios.

Proportion: $\dfrac{1}{2} = \dfrac{3}{4}$ Alternate Proportion: $\dfrac{1}{3} = \dfrac{2}{4}$

Alternate Proportions

The proportion 7 : 10 = 35 : 50 is true. Write the alternate proportion and use cross products to show it is true.

Step 1: The original proportion is

$$7 : 10 = 35 : 50 \quad \text{or} \quad \frac{7}{10} = \frac{35}{50}$$

Write the alternate proportion. The first set of corresponding terms, 7 and 35, becomes the first ratio. The second set of corresponding terms, 10 and 50, becomes the second ratio.

$$\frac{7}{35} = \frac{10}{50}$$

Step 2: Cross multiply.

$$7 \times 50 = 35 \times 10$$
$$350 = 350$$

The cross products are equal, so the proportion is true.

TEST TIME: Multiple Choice

The proportion A : B = C : D is true.
What other proportion must also be true?

   a. A : D = B : C
   b. B : A = C : D
   c. A : C = B : D
   d. A : C = D : B

The alternate proportion is A : C = B : D. Other true proportions compare the reciprocal of each of the ratios, B : A = D : C, or change the left and right sides of the equal sign, C : D = A : B.

Solution: The correct answer is c.

Test-Taking Hint

Put a small mark next to answers you're not sure of. When you finish your test, go back and check those problems first.

14. Percents

Ratios and Percents

Jason has $100. He spent $16 on a new headlight for his car. What percent of Jason's money did he spend on the headlight?

Step 1: Write the ratio of dollars spent on the headlight to total dollars.

$$16 : 100$$

Step 2: When the second term of a ratio is 100, it can be written as a percent by replacing the second term with a percent sign.

$$16\%$$

Jason spent 16% of his money on the headlight.

TEST TIME: Show Your Work

One hundred chairs were inspected for quality. One hundred chairs passed the inspection. What percent of the chairs passed the inspection?

The ratio of chairs that passed to total chairs is 100 to 100. As a percent, this is 100%. Any time the first and second term of a ratio are the same, the ratio can be written as 100%. You do not need to show any computations. Remember to write the answer in a complete sentence.

Solution: 100% of the chairs passed the inspection.

Test-Taking Hint

Work at your own pace. Don't worry about how fast anyone else is taking the same test.

Writing Percents as Ratios

Write 27% and 113% as ratios.

Step 1: Write 27% as a ratio. The first term of the ratio is the number part of a percent.

$$27:$$

Step 2: The second term of the ratio is always 100.

$$27:100$$

Step 3: Write 113% in the same way. The first term of the ratio is the number part of the percent. The second term is always 100.

$$113:100$$

Test-Taking Hint

Reduce to lowest terms to get full credit on test problems whenever it is appropriate.

TEST TIME: Multiple Choice

In Sarai's class, 72% of the students had summer jobs.
What ratio of the students had summer jobs to students in the class?

          a. 18 : 25
          b. 3 : 4
          c. 7 : 10
          d. 37 : 50

Write the ratio using the number part of the percent as the first term and 100 as the second term. 72 : 100

Reduce the ratio to lowest terms if it can be reduced. Each term can be divided by 2.

$$72 \div 2 : 100 \div 2$$
$$36 : 50$$

The terms still have a common factor. Divide each term by 2 again.

$$36 \div 2 : 50 \div 2$$
$$18 : 25$$

Solution: The correct answer is a.

15. Fractions, Decimals, and Percents

Rewriting Percents

Percents can be written as fractions or decimals.

Write 87% as a fraction.

Step 1: Percents are written as fractions that have a denominator of 100. The percentage, or number part of the percent, is the numerator.

$$\frac{87}{100}$$

$$87\% = \frac{87}{100}$$

Write 27% as a decimal.

Step 1: Percents are written as decimals by dropping the percent sign and moving the decimal point two places left.

$$27\%$$
$$0.27$$

$$27\% = 0.27$$

TEST TIME: Show Your Work

Kyle found that 20% of the sixth grade students in his school have cell phones. What is 20% as a decimal and a fraction?

Solution: Write the percent as a decimal by dropping the percent sign and moving the decimal point two places left.

20% = 0.20

Write the percent as a fraction by using the percentage as the numerator and 100 as the denominator. Reduce the fraction to lowest terms.

$$20\% = \frac{20}{100} = \frac{20 \div 20}{100 \div 20} = \frac{1}{5}$$

$$20\% = 0.20 \text{ and } \frac{1}{5}$$

TEST TIME: Multiple Choice

12.7 = _____

        a. 0.127%

        b. 12.7%

        c. 127%

        d. 1270%

Decimals are written as percents by multiplying the decimal by 100 and adding a percent sign. Multiplying a number by 100 moves the decimal point two places right.

12.7 = 1270%

Solution: The correct answer is d.

Writing Fractions as Percents

You can use more than one method to change a fraction to a percent.

Jess ate exactly $\frac{1}{2}$ of her doughnut and gave the rest to her sister. What percent of the doughnut did Jess eat?

One way: You can change a fraction to a percent by multiplying the fraction by 100 and adding the percent sign.

$$\frac{1}{2} \times 100 = \frac{1}{2} \times \frac{100}{1} = \frac{100}{2} = \frac{50}{1} = 50$$

$$\frac{1}{2} = 50\%$$

Another way: Write the fraction as a decimal by dividing the numerator by the denominator.

$$1 \div 2 = 0.5$$

Change the decimal to a percent by moving the decimal point two places right and adding the percent sign.

$$0.5 = 50\%$$

Calculator Tip

A calculator is a useful tool when converting fractions to decimals. Divide the numerator by the denominator to find the decimal or to check your calculations.

Percent Problems

Percent problems relate a percent, a part, and a whole. You can solve a percent problem by setting up a proportion. One ratio is the percent (with 100 as the second term). The other ratio is a part to a whole.

What is 25% of 28?

Step 1: Set up the proportion. You know the percentage is 25. You must decide if 28 is a part or a whole. You want to know what part of 28 is 25%. This means 28 is the whole.

$$\frac{percentage}{100} = \frac{part}{whole}$$

$$\frac{25}{100} = \frac{?}{28}$$

Step 2: Solve the proportion. Cross multiply the terms you know. Divide by the term that is left.

$$25 \times 28 = 700$$
$$700 \div 100 = 7$$

$$\frac{25}{100} = \frac{7}{28}$$

25% of 28 is 7.

Test-Taking Hint

Use the statement "percent of whole is part" to help you decide what numbers are the part and whole. In the problem on page 66, 25% (percent) of 28 (whole) is 7 (part).

TEST TIME: Multiple Choice

What percent of 20 is 8?

     a. 4%

     b. 16%

     c. 20%

     d. 40%

This problem is asking for the percentage. Set up a proportion. For the part to whole ratio, 8 is the part and 20 is the whole.

$$\frac{percentage}{100} = \frac{8}{20}$$

Cross multiply and divide. $8 \times 100 = 800$

                                  $800 \div 20 = 40$

8 is 40% of 20.

Solution: The correct answer is d.

TEST TIME: Show Your Work

Madi's basketball team scored 60 points in their last game. The table below shows how many points each girl scored. What percent of the total points were scored by girls who have names starting with M?

Name	Points
Abigal	0
Maureen	12
Greta	6
Madi	6
Julie	10
Emilie	24
Catherine	2

Some of the information you need to solve a problem may be given in a table, graph, chart, or picture. This problem requires you to find the number of points scored by girls who have names that start with M before you can find the percentage.

Two girls have names that start with M. Add to find their points together. Set up and solve a proportion to find the percentage.

Solution: Maureen's points + Madi's points = 12 + 6 = 18

Total points (given in the problem) = 60

$$\frac{\text{percentage}}{100} = \frac{18}{60}$$

Cross multiply and divide. $18 \times 100 = 1800$

$$1800 \div 60 = 30$$

30% of the points were scored by girls who have names that start with M.

Test-Taking Hint

Make notes in your test booklet to help you solve problems. For the problem on the previous page, you can make small marks next to the girls who have a name that starts with M.

Percents and Money

How much will you save if you buy a sweater that is marked 35% off $50.00?

Step 1: Set up a proportion. This problem uses the ratio of savings (part) to original price (whole).

$$\frac{percentage}{100} = \frac{part}{whole}$$

$$\frac{35}{100} = \frac{?}{\$50.00}$$

Step 2: Solve the proportion. Treat money values like any other decimal. Cross multiply the terms you know. Divide by the term that is left.

$$35 \times \$50.00 = \$1750.00$$
$$\$1750.00 \div 100 = \$17.50$$

Step 3: Write the answer. Be sure to include the dollar sign and decimal point when your answer is a money value.

You will save $17.50 on the sweater.

17. The Percent Equation

Definition

the percent equation: An equation that relates percent, whole, and part. The statement "percent of whole is part" is written as the equation percent × whole = part.

Percent of a Number

What is 23% of 200?

Step 1: Write the percent equation. Replace the words in the equation with the numbers that you know. You know the percent and the whole.

$$\text{percent} \times \text{whole} = \text{part}$$
$$23\% \times 200 = \text{part}$$

Step 2: To use a percent in an equation, write it as a decimal or a fraction. Move the decimal point two places left to write the percent as a decimal.

$$0.23 \times 200 = \text{part}$$

Step 3: Multiply.

$$0.23 \times 200 = 46$$

23% of 200 is 46.

TEST TIME: Show Your Work

A $60.00 jacket is marked 30% off.
What is the sale price of the jacket?

This problem can be solved in two steps. First, find the amount that is being taken off the original price using the percent equation. Then, subtract that amount from the original price.

Solution: Write the percent equation.   percent × whole = part
Put in the numbers you know.   30% × $60.00 = part
Write the percent as a decimal. 0.30 × $60.00 = part
Multipy.   0.30 × $60.00 = $18.00

$18.00 is being taken off the original price.
Subtract to find the sale price. $60.00 − $18.00 = $42.00

The sale price of the jacket is $42.00.

Test-Taking Hint

Read problems carefully. Decide how you can use the information given to solve the problem.

TEST TIME: Explain Your Answer

To find 25% of 8, is it easier to change the percent to a fraction or a decimal? Explain your decision.

Solution: I would find it easier to change 25% to a fraction for this problem. 25% is the same as 0.25 or 1/4.

To find 25% of 8, I would use the percent equation.

$$25\% \times 8 = ?$$

I can multiply 1/4 × 8 using mental math, for a product of 2.

0.25 × 8 is too hard for me to multiply mentally.

Test-Taking Hint

"Explain your answer" questions may have different answers and still be correct, as long as you can explain your reasoning.

Fractional Percents

A percentage can be a fraction, such as 1/4%, or a decimal, such as 0.575%.

What is 1/2% of 80?

Step 1: Write the percent as a fraction or a decimal.
To write a fractional percent as a fraction, divide the percent by 100.

$$\frac{1}{2}\% - \frac{1}{2} \div 100 = \frac{1}{2} \times \frac{1}{100} = \frac{1}{200}$$

To write a fractional percent as a decimal, change the fractional percent to a decimal percent first. Then change the decimal percent to a decimal.

$$\frac{1}{2}\% = 0.5\% = 0.005$$

Step 2: Use the percent equation to solve the problem.

$$\text{percent} \times \text{whole} = \text{part}$$

$$\frac{1}{2}\% \times 80 = \text{part}$$

$$\frac{1}{200} \times 80 = \frac{1}{200} \times \frac{80}{1} = \frac{80}{200} = \frac{2}{5}$$

OR $\quad \frac{1}{2}\% \times 80 = \text{part}$

$$0.005 \times 80 = 0.4$$

$$\frac{1}{2}\% \text{ of } 80 \text{ is } \frac{2}{5} \text{ or } 0.4.$$

18. Percents Over 100%

Exactly 100%

In a percent problem, when the part is equal to the whole it is 100%.

There were 27 jelly beans in a jar. Armanda ate 100% of them. How many jelly beans did Armanda eat?

Step 1: Write the percent equation. The original number of jelly beans is the whole. Replace the words in the equation with the numbers that you know.

$$\textbf{percent} \times \textbf{whole} = \textbf{part}$$
$$\textbf{100\%} \times \textbf{27} = \textbf{part}$$

Step 2: Write 100% as a decimal. Move the decimal point two places left.

$$\textbf{1.00} \times \textbf{27} = \textbf{part}$$

Step 3: Multiply.

$$\textbf{1.00} \times \textbf{27} = \textbf{27}$$

Armanda ate 27 jelly beans.

100% of any number is exactly that number.
100% of 27 is 27.

TEST TIME: Show Your Work

Last year season passes for football games cost $20 per person. This year season passes cost 200% of what they did last year. How much are this year's season passes?

This problem can be solved using paper and pencil or mental math. Because it is a "show your work" problem, use paper and pencil.

Solution: Write the percent equation.   percent × whole = part

Put in the numbers you know.   200% × $20 = part

Write the percent as a decimal.   2.00 × $20 = part

Multipy.   2.00 × $20 = $40

This year's season passes are $40.

Does this answer make sense? 200% is twice as much as 100%. If 100% of $20 is $20, then 200% is twice as much, or $40. Yes, this answer makes sense.

Greater Than the Whole

When a percent is greater than 100%, the part is greater than the whole.

What is 125% of 60?

Step 1: Let's use a proportion to solve this problem. You know the percentage is 125. The whole is 60.

$$\frac{\text{percentage}}{100} = \frac{\text{part}}{\text{whole}}$$

$$\frac{125}{100} = \frac{?}{60}$$

Step 2: Solve the proportion. Cross multiply the terms you know. Divide by the term that is left.

$$125 \times 60 = 7{,}500$$
$$7{,}500 \div 100 = 75$$

$$\frac{125}{100} = \frac{75}{60}$$

125% of 60 is 75.

Let's check this using the percent equation.

$$\text{percent} \times \text{whole} = \text{part}$$
$$125\% \times 60 = 75$$
$$1.25 \times 60 = 75$$
$$75 = 75$$

TEST TIME: Multiple Choice

Nigel set a goal of walking 6 miles for the week. His actual distance walked was 160% of his goal. How far did Nigel walk?

> a. 3.6 miles
> b. 6.0 miles
> c. 8.0 miles
> d. 9.6 miles

Use the percent equation.

$$\text{percent} \times \text{whole} = \text{part}$$
$$160\% \times 6 = ?$$
$$1.6 \times 6 = 9.6$$

9.6 is greater than 6.

This makes sense since 160% is greater than 100%.

Solution: The correct answer is d.

19. Finding a Percentage

Ratios as Percents

A package of 30 sheets of colored cardstock contains 6 sheets of pink cardstock. What percent of the package is pink?

Step 1: Write the ratio of pink sheets to total sheets.

$$\frac{6}{30}$$

Step 2: Write the ratio as a decimal. Divide the first term by the second term.

$$6 \div 30 = 0.2$$

Step 3: Write the decimal as a percent by moving the decimal two places right and adding the percent sign.

$$0.2 = 20\%$$

20% of the package is pink.

The numbers from the problem above can be written in the percent equation.

$$20\% \times 30 = 6$$

TEST TIME: Multiple Choice

What percent of 90 is 72?

      a. 36%
      b. 45%
      c. 80%
      d. 125%

Use the statement "percent of a whole is a part" to decide that 90 is the whole and 72 is the part. The whole is larger than the part, so you know answer d is not correct. You can also eliminate answers a and b by knowing that 72 is more than half (50%) of 90. There is no need to do any actual computation for this problem.

Solution: The correct answer is c.

Use the percent equation to check answer c.
$$80\% \times 90 = 72$$
$$0.8 \times 90 = 72$$
$$72 = 72$$

Use a Proportion

What percent of 9 is 6?

Step 1: You can use a proportion to understand how to find a percentage. Set up the proportion with the percent ratio on one side of the equation.

$$\frac{\text{percentage}}{100} = \frac{\text{part}}{\text{whole}}$$

$$\frac{?}{100} = \frac{6}{9}$$

Step 2: Solve the proportion. Cross multiply the terms you know. Divide by the term that is left.

$$100 \times 6 = 600$$
$$600 \div 9 = 66\,{}^{2}/_{3}$$

Remember, percentages can be written as fractions or decimals. In this case, the decimal would $66.\overline{6}$. Instead of writing a repeating decimal, use a fractional answer.

6 is 66 ${}^{2}/_{3}$% of 9.

Test-Taking Hint

When you use a calculator, you still need to understand what to do with the numbers in the problem. A calculator is only a tool, not a problem-solver.

TEST TIME: Show Your Work

Out of 850 students at DeSales High School, 34 were late for classes on Friday. What percent of the students were late on Friday?

You can write a ratio and then change it to a percentage, or write and solve a proportion to find the percentage. Let's write a ratio.

Solution: The ratio of late students to total students is $\dfrac{34}{850}$.

Change the ratio to a decimal by dividing the first term by the second term. You can use a calculator to do the division.

$$34 \times 850 = 0.04$$

Write the decimal as a percent.

$$0.04 = 4\%$$

4% of the students at DeSales High School were late on Friday.

20. Finding a Whole

Use a Proportion

A proportion can be used to solve any percent problem. You can find the part, the whole, or the percent by setting up and solving a proportion.

90% of ___ is 54.

Step 1: You can use a proportion to understand how to find a percentage. Set up the proportion with the percent ratio on one side of the equation.

$$\frac{\text{percentage}}{100} = \frac{\text{part}}{\text{whole}}$$

$$\frac{90}{100} = \frac{54}{?}$$

Step 2: Solve the proportion. Cross multiply the terms you know. Divide by the term that is left.

$$100 \times 54 = 5{,}400$$
$$5{,}400 \div 90 = 60$$

90% of 60 is 54.

Test-Taking Hint

Be careful to avoid careless answers on easy questions. Focus on each problem, and don't be in a hurry.

TEST TIME: Multiple Choice

The results of a survey showed that 64% of women between 25 and 30 use a facial moisturizer. Of those surveyed, 96 women said they used a facial moisturizer. How many women took the survey?

     a. 61
     b. 96
     ⓒ 150
     d. 160

Write a proportion.
$$\frac{64}{100} = \frac{96}{?}$$

Cross multiply and divide.
$$100 \times 96 = 9{,}600$$
$$9{,}600 \div 64 = 150$$

150 women took the survey.

Solution: The correct answer is c.

The Percent Equation

The percent equation, along with inverse operations, can be used to solve any percent problem.

50% of ___ is 18.

Step 1: Write the percent equation. Replace the words in the equation with the numbers that you know.

$$\text{percent} \times \text{whole} = \text{part}$$
$$50\% \times \text{whole} = 18$$

Step 2: Write the percent as a decimal.

$$0.5 \times \underline{\quad} = 18$$

Step 3: Use inverse operations to write the multiplication equation as a division equation.

$$18 \div 0.5 = \underline{\quad}$$

Step 4: Divide. You can use a calculator, or paper and pencil. When you divide by a decimal, make the decimal a whole number by moving the decimal point the same number of places in each number.

$$18 \div 0.5 = \underline{\quad}$$
$$180 \div 5 = 36$$

50% of 36 is 18.

TEST TIME: Show Your Work

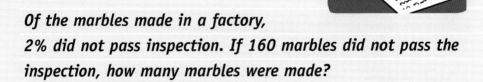

*Of the marbles made in a factory,
2% did not pass inspection. If 160 marbles did not pass the
inspection, how many marbles were made?*

Use the percent equation and inverse operations to find the
total number of marbles made.

Solution: Write the percent equation.   percent $\times$ whole = part

Put in the numbers you know.   2% $\times$ ____ = 160

Write the percent as a decimal.   0.02 $\times$ ____ = 160

Rewrite multiplication as division. 160 $\div$ 0.02 = ___

Divide.   160 $\div$ 0.02 = 8,000

8,000 marbles were made.

Test-Taking Hint

Multiplication and division are inverse operations.
Any multiplication equation can be written as a
division equation, and vice versa.

$3 \times 4 = 12$ is the same as $12 \div 4 = 3$.

21. Percent of Change

Definitions

percent of change: The ratio, written as a percent, of the amount of change to an original amount.

percent of increase: The percent of change when a new value is larger than the original value.

percent of decrease: The percent of change when a new value is less than the original value.

Percent of Increase

This quarter Tracy is taking 4 hours of class time more than she did last quarter. She took 20 hours of classes last quarter. What is the percent of increase in Tracy's hours of class time?

Step 1: This problem tells you Tracy's class time has increased, or changed, by 4 hours. Write a ratio that compares the amount of change, 4 hours, to the original number of hours, 20.

$$\frac{\text{change}}{\text{original}} \qquad \frac{4}{20}$$

Step 2: Write the ratio as a percent. Divide. Then write the decimal as a percent.

$$4 \div 20 = 0.2$$
$$0.2 = 20\%$$

The percent of increase in Tracy's class hours was 20%.

TEST TIME: Show Your Work

During the summer, the cost of heating fuel was $1.60 per gallon. In the winter, the rate changed to $2.08 per gallon. What was the percent of increase in the cost of fuel?

Solution: The percent of increase compares the amount the cost changed to the original cost. To find the amount the cost changed, subtract the old cost from the new cost.

$$\$2.08 - \$1.60 = \$0.48$$

The cost of a gallon of fuel increased by $0.48.
Write the ratio of change to original cost.

$$\$0.48/\$1.60.$$

Divide. $\qquad \$0.48 \div \$1.60 = 0.30,$ or 30%.

The percent of increase in the cost of fuel was 30%.

Test-Taking Hint

Some problems require more than one step. In the problem above, you must find the difference in the summer and winter costs before you can find the percent of increase.

Percent of Decrease

The price of a chess set in a consignment shop is changed from $8 to $5. What is the percent of decrease?

Step 1: Find the difference in the original price and the new price.

$$\$8 - \$5 = \$3$$

Step 1: Write a ratio that compares the amount of change, $3 to the original price, $8.

$$\frac{\text{change}}{\text{original}} \qquad \frac{\$3}{\$8}$$

Step 2: Write the ratio as a percent. Divide. Then write the decimal as a percent.

$$3 \div 8 = 0.375$$
$$0.375 = 37.5\%$$

The percent of decrease in the price of the chess set was 37.5%.

Test-Taking Hint

Remember to include the units, like hours or feet, in your answers. In a problem that requires writing, use complete sentences.

TEST TIME: Explain Your Answer

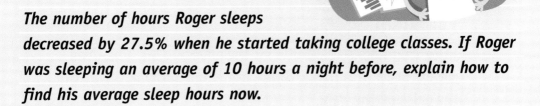

The number of hours Roger sleeps decreased by 27.5% when he started taking college classes. If Roger was sleeping an average of 10 hours a night before, explain how to find his average sleep hours now.

Solution: You know that the percent of change is the ratio of the change to the original. This can be written as an equation.

$$\text{percent of change} = \text{change/original}$$

Put the number you are given into the equation.

$$27.5\% = \text{change}/10$$

or

$$0.275 = \text{change} \div 10$$

This can be rewritten as the multiplication equation. Then multiply.

$$0.275 \times 10 = \text{change}$$
$$2.75 = \text{change (hours)}$$

This problem asks about the average sleep Roger gets now. You know how much sleep he was getting, and you know it has decreased by 2.75 hours. Subtract to find how many hours he averages now.

$$10 \text{ hours} - 2.75 \text{ hours} = 7.25 \text{ hours}$$

Roger now gets an average of 7.25 hours of sleep a night.

Definition

sales tax: Money collected by the government when you purchase certain items. Sales tax is normally a percent of the price of the item.

Sales Tax

How much is an 8% sales tax on a $32.00 quilt?

Step 1: Finding the amount of sales tax is done just like any other percent problem. Write the percent equation.

$$\text{percent} \times \text{whole} = \text{part}$$
$$8\% \times \$32.00 = \text{sales tax}$$

Step 2: Write the percent as a decimal.

$$0.08 \times \$32.00 = \text{sales tax}$$

Step 3: Multiply.

$$\$2.56 = \text{sales tax}$$

An 8% sales tax on a $32.00 quilt is $2.56.

TEST TIME: Multiple Choice

What is the total cost of an $80.00 computer chair that has a 5.75% sales tax?

a. $4.60
b. $75.40
c. $84.60
d. $126.00

Find the amount of sales tax and add it to the cost of the chair to find the total cost.

5.75% × $80.00 = 0.0575 × $80.00 = $4.60

$80.00 + $4.60 = $84.60

Solution: The correct answer is c.

Test-Taking Hint

Read word problems carefully. Key words such as total, per, average, or difference can help you decide what operation should be performed. This problem uses the word total to indicate addition.

Definition

discount: The amount that is taken off the original price of an item. A discount can be a dollar amount or a percent of the original price.

Discount

Employees of a restaurant get a 15% discount on any food they purchase. For a total bill of $28.00, what is the amount of the discount?

Step 1: Finding the amount of a discount is done just like any other percent problem. Write the percent equation.

$$\textbf{percent} \times \textbf{whole} = \textbf{part}$$
$$\textbf{15\%} \times \textbf{\$28.00} = \textbf{discount}$$

Step 2: Write the percent as a decimal.

$$\textbf{0.15} \times \textbf{\$28.00} = \textbf{discount}$$

Step 3: Multiply.

$$\textbf{\$4.20} = \textbf{discount}$$

A 15% discount on a $28.00 bill is $4.20.

TEST TIME: Show Your Work

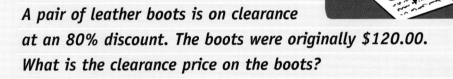

A pair of leather boots is on clearance at an 80% discount. The boots were originally $120.00. What is the clearance price on the boots?

This problem can be solved in two different ways. You can find the amount of the discount, and subtract it from the original price. Or you can understand that if the boots are discounted 80%, the new price is 20% of the original price.

Solution: Find the discount. 80% of $120.00 is the discount.

$$80\% \times \$120.00 = \text{discount}$$
$$0.8 \times \$120.00 = \$96.00$$

Subtract discount from original price. $120.00 - \$96.00 = \$24.00$

The clearance price of the boots is $24.00.

Check your answer by finding 20% of the original price.
20% of $120.00 = 20\% \times \$120.00 = 0.2 \times \$120.00 = \$24.00$

Test-Taking Hint

Check your answers whenever you can. In the problem above, you can check your answer by solving the problem another way.

23. Tips

TEST TIME: Explain Your Answer

Multiply $25.00 by 100%, by 10%, and by 1%. Explain any patterns you see.

Solution: $25.00 × 100% = $25.00 × 1 = $25.00

$25.00 × 10% = $25.00 × 0.1 = $2.50

$25.00 × 1% = $25.00 × 0.01 = $0.25

In each equation, the digits stayed the same. The only difference was the location of the decimal point. For each decimal place in the power of 10, the decimal point moves one place left in the product.

Test-Taking Hint

Multiplication by a decimal power of ten (e.g., 0.1, 0.01, 0.001 . . .) moves the decimal point to the left. Multiplication by a whole number power of ten (e.g., 10, 100, 1,000 . . .) moves the decimal point to the right.

Definition

tip: An amount of money given to show appreciation for a service. For example, you might tip a waiter or a hairdresser. Tips are often given as a percent of the cost of the service.

Tips

Melanie had her hair cut for $50.00. She wants to tip her hairdresser 10%. How much money should her tip be?

Step 1: Write the percent equation. Change the percent to a decimal.

$$10\% \times \$50.00 = \text{tip}$$
$$0.1 \times \$50.00 = \text{tip}$$

Step 2: You can multiply by a decimal power of 10 using mental math. There is one decimal place in 0.1. Move the decimal point one place left.

$$0.1 \times \$50.00 = \$5.00$$

Melanie should give the hairdresser a $5.00 tip.

Definition

estimate: An answer that is not exact. A good estimate is an answer that is close to the exact answer.

TEST TIME: Show Your Work

Piers wants to tip a waiter about 15% on a total bill of $64.75. About how much should he tip?

A tip does not need to be an exact amount or even an exact percent. Estimation is used often in tipping, so the tip is an even dollar amount.

Solution: Round $64.75 to the nearest whole dollar.

$64.75 is about $65.00

Find 15% of $65.00.

15% × $65.00 = $9.75

Piers should tip about $9.75.
To tip a whole dollar amount, Piers could tip $10.00.

TEST TIME: Multiple Choice

For a 30% tip on a $15.00 service, how much should you tip?

        a. $3.50

        b. $4.00

        c. $4.50

        d. $6.50

You can use mental math to calculate many tips. Think: How much is 10% of $15.00? $1.50. 30% is three times as much as 10%. $1.50 + $1.50 + $1.50 = $4.50

Solution: The correct answer is c.

Test-Taking Hint

You can go through a test and do the easy problems first. This can help you gain confidence, and keeps you from running out of time and missing easy points.

24. Simple Interest

Definitions

principal: The amount of money in an account.

interest rate: The percent that is paid by the borrower.

simple interest: Interest that is found one time on the principal. The formula for finding simple interest is

$$\text{interest} = \text{principal} \times \text{rate} \times \text{time}$$

Simple Interest

Dan borrowed $1,000 for 2 years at a simple interest rate of 5%. How much interest did he pay?

Step 1: Use the formula for simple interest. Fill in the amounts you know.

$$\text{interest} = \text{principal} \times \text{rate} \times \text{time}$$
$$\text{interest} = \$1000 \times 5\% \times 2 \text{ years}$$

Step 2: Change the percent to a decimal. Interest is calculated in years.

$$\text{interest} = \$1000 \times 0.05 \times 2$$

Step 3: Multiply.

$$\text{interest} = \$1000 \times (0.05 \times 2)$$
$$\text{interest} = \$1000 \times 0.1$$
$$\text{interest} = \$100$$

Dan paid $100 in interest.

TEST TIME: Multiple Choice

What is the simple interest on $2,640.00 over 3 years at 4.5%?

a. $35.64
b. $118.80
c. $356.40
d. $1,188.00

When the numbers are difficult to calculate quickly, use a calculator as a tool.

interest = principal × rate × time
interest = $2640.00 × 4.5% × 3
interest = $2640.00 × 0.045 × 3 = $356.40

Solution: The correct answer is c.

Test-Taking Hint

Know your calculator. If you're using someone else's calculator, make sure you understand how to use it before you begin a test.

Semiannual Interest

Interest is found using time in terms of years. When using the interest formula, convert all time units into years.

Find the semiannual interest on a loan of $500.00 at 6%.

Step 1: Write the equation for simple interest. Fill in the amounts you know. Semiannual means every six months.

$$\text{interest} = \text{principal} \times \text{rate} \times \text{time}$$
$$\text{interest} = \$500.00 \times 6\% \times 6 \text{ months}$$

Step 2: Change the percent to a decimal. Interest is calculated in years. Six months is the same as half a year, or 0.5 years.

$$\text{interest} = \$500.00 \times 0.06 \times 0.5$$

Step 3: Multiply.

$$\text{interest} = \$500.00 \times (0.06 \times 0.5)$$
$$\text{interest} = \$500.00 \times 0.03$$
$$\text{interest} = \$15.00$$

The semiannual interest on the loan is $15.00.

TEST TIME: Show Your Work

Pat borrowed $4,000.00 for three months at a simple interest rate of 10%. How much did Pat have to pay back in total on the loan?

This problem does not ask how much the interest is on the loan. It does ask how much Pat must pay back in total. The total to repay the loan includes the original loan and the interest.

Solution: Find the interest. interest = principal × rate × time

interest = $4000.00 × 10% × 3 months

The interest is found for a period of three months. Three months is the same as 3 out of 12 months, or 3 ÷ 12. 3 ÷ 12 = 0.25

interest = $4000.00 × 0.1 × 0.25

interest = $100.00

original loan interest = $4000.00 + $100.00 = $4,100.00

Pat had to repay $4,100.00 total on the loan.

Test-Taking Hint

Make sure you are answering the question that is asked. This problem asks for the total amount to repay.

Further Reading

Books

Adler, David A. *Fractions, Decimals, and Percents.* New York: Holiday House, 2010.

McKellar, Danica. *Math Doesn't Suck: How to Survive Middle School Math Without Losing Your Mind or Breaking a Nail.* New York: Hudson Street Press, 2007.

Rozakis, Laurie. *Get Test Smart!: The Ultimate Guide to Middle School Standardized Tests.* New York: Scholastic Reference, 2007.

Internet Addresses

Banfill, J. **AAA Math.** "Ratios." 2009.
http://www.aaamath.com/rat.htm

Coolmath.com, Inc. **Percent Lessons.** 1997–2010.
http://www.coolmath.com/prealgebra/03-percents/index.html

Testtakingtips.com. **Test Taking Tips.** 2003–2010.
http://www.testtakingtips.com/test/math.htm

Index

Index